POETRY

SERIES

$2.25
POET

Jack Anderson

The Invention
of New Jersey

EXIT

The Invention of New Jersey

Poems by JACK ANDERSON

The Invention of
New Jersey

University of Pittsburgh Press

Library of Congress Catalog Card Number 69–12328

Manufactured in the United States of America

Acknowledgment is made to the following periodicals and books in which some of these poems first appeared: *The American Literary Anthology* (Random House), *Antioch Review, Bones, Chelsea, Choice, Colorado Quarterly, Elephant, Epoch, For Now, Genesis West, Hanging Loose, Lines, The Nation, Noose, Poetmeat, Riverrun, San Francisco Review, Silo, Sun, 31 New American Poets* (Hill and Wang), *University of Tampa Poetry Review*, and *The World*. "The Invention of New Jersey" was awarded an endowment by the National Council on the Arts.

Contents

The Invention of New Jersey

A Waking

At dawn the world has not yet decided
its color.
            And so
to us in unfinished
love, precarious
juncture,
glass on the shelf's edge.
                    Mouldering
vows stay us: crumbs of stars in their cupboards.
At arm's reach, passions sorted in cannisters
like a Dutch pantry, the
confections of waking.
                    Day
comes red, yellow: no marzipan
sweet paste, but sharp
cinnamon.

Some days it happens that people fall in love
because it is Saturday and they have seen Greek statues
so it happens while everyone else is eating or on the subway

and they look up from a newspaper and say
"O sweet lying mazurkas ground by the wheels!"
and they rustle their newspapers with joy conversing

"O sweet lying stranger let us lie here together"
"you are false as an angel but let us empty our pockets"
"let our coins and our weapons lie side by side"

"in the sky the moon slobbers and makes a pig of itself"

In the Next Room

It is raining.
In the next room someone
Reads in a low voice.

Sleep is very warm here.
A light across the road
Flickers on and off.
Music from a phonograph
Hangs in the distance
Like faded wallpaper.

Odor of evergreen.
Odor of rain.
Here nothing is lacking
And our eyes converse.
In the next room someone
Stretches cold water
Against his lips.

The body on the bed
Presses close to itself.

Napoleon's Retreat

The Queen of Hearts is waltzing on the ice. She wears a sealskin coat and a bonnet of ptarmigan feathers. Napoleon has deserted her.

It is a month between December and January. Christmas has been burned to the ground. The Queen of Hearts is waltzing on the frozen pond. Her boots are the color of otter's milk. Her muff is made of the fur of wolves. Distant cannon fire shakes the ice.

Napoleon has deserted her. Napoleon has deserted her like a monarch who cringes from the hawk on his wrist. With the departure of Napoleon on his belly, on his naked belly, on his frostbitten naked belly dragged through the snow, the bells begin to peal and a hidden chorus sings Beethoven's Ninth Symphony.

The Queen of Hearts circles in figure-eights and cries, "All my heroes leave me. They leave my knuckles, my elbows, my tongue. The heroes go home or soliloquize before their horses. I try to keep them with my knees, my breasts, the lobes of my ears, my toes, my mouth, my teeth. But they fall like mice against my anklebones. They limp like wounded rabbits through tunnels in dead stumps. My heroes limp home supported by their faithful drummer boys."

Napoleon crawls with cannon smoke along the highroad. Napoleon's lieutenants (who are all Napoleon), Napoleon's sergeants (who are all Napoleon), Napoleon's privates (who are all Napoleon) crawl through the snow which reminds them of old surgical dressings. "Hunger! Hunger!" cry the hawks. "Bones! Bones!" cry the bones in the steel traps. "Joy! Joy!" cry Beethoven and the Polytechnical Institute Glee Club. Then silence falls like snow. Snow falls like teeth. Teeth shine like hatpins. The Queen of Hearts is telling the story of her life. The New Year falls like the New Year.

The village band on the municipal pier strikes up a waltz with trombones. In a thawed place the drummer boys are dancing with the dairymaids. The Trans-Siberian Railroad arrives at Sun Valley. A widow who teaches algebra pours hot buttered rum for Napoleon. The Queen of Hearts is thin as paper. She keeps turning like paper in the wind. Her fingernails have grown very long.

The Princess of Feet-Above-Sea-Level

The Princess of Feet-Above-Sea-Level
is coming is going is about to arrive
is slowly drawing her little finger
in semicircles across the barometer
at the airdrome the windsocks
are worn by the wind

The Princess of Feet-Above-Sea-Level
drones like a tortoise on a long safari
is shelling peas her little finger
tracing circles of damp on the rim of a dish
apples the winesaps the Muscovy ducks
fall fall are falling / to arrive

Airdromes like a tortoise or pumps under snow
the witch with the ague in the weather house
the rime on the dish presses circles of damp
the fur of the seal / the pressure of freezing
arrive with the Princess of Feet-Above-Sea-Level
in the inn with the chamois head caught in the wall

At the hearth the Princess of Feet-Above-Sea-Level
savors plum pudding with wind in the chimney
nor horse nor seahorse nor tusk of the boar
nor quadrant nor witch with the dropsy can trace
her coming her going her about to arrive
in the milk pail frozen / in the drone of the well

The Dread

The street brightens and fades / brightens and fades.
A horse races through me.
He pulls a hundred carriages behind him.
The wheels spin in the ditches.

The street brightens and fades / brightens and fades.
Pages fall from calendars.
They knot themselves between my teeth.
Sand runs from the faucets.

A horse races through a wall inside me.
His legs flutter like paper.
He drinks only the foam on his lips.
He pulls a hundred sealed carriages behind him.

The street brightens and fades / brightens and fades.
And numbers taste like blood in my mouth.

Ceremony of Departure

The woman at the window repeated, "It's four o'clock."
The suitcases I pack
are bottomless,
to be stuffed with buttons
and endless spools of thread.

The woman at the window repeated, "It's four o'clock,"
and recited the itinerary.
The clasps on the luggage sprang open.
Old teeth, strands of hair, bitten nails
litter the street.

My shadow leaps before me
as I cross the square.
As I pass under the arches
another row of arches
leaps ahead.

The hands tremble on the clock.
I have forgotten my papers,
my portmanteau, my valise.
Women come to the windows.
"It's four o'clock," they say.

The warning bell rings in the terminal.
The women throw passports like roses.
I run but the buildings beside me
do not move, do not move.
The gate slides shut at the platform
and the windows are empty, boarded, soaped.

Fiction

You, who have always relished the picturesque, may be interested to learn that our life here has become identical to a page of fiction.

On the surface, little seems changed. We still go about our business, and it is our business to go about looking well. But the very act of getting about has grown harder because there are generators blowing strong winds in our paths, so that wherever we go we confront the wind which hardens into despair on our faces. Of course, no one admits that it bothers him—for who would dare hint that he is lacking in confidence? All the same, we do not go out as much as we once did.

An invisible war has been placed inside the air which, instead of killing us outright, is gradually draining us. Even stone buildings are being drained. We have been told that there is another war someplace else, a visible war from which we are being spared. But to keep it invisible requires great energy; in fact, the very energy that is being siphoned out of us. We can be thankful for at least one thing: it does not hurt. Yet we are now no stronger than paper. In a short time all of us will collapse with hardly a sound—whole families, whole streets, even whole cities collapsing with only a faint, delicate rustle.

In the meantime, there is nothing to complain of. Except for the smell of burning which afflicts us. It is very strong, comes from no identifiable source, and is all-pervasive. It is quite impossible to ignore. But some people develop a tolerance to it and there are even those who profess to thrive on it.

The final inconvenience here is the ambulatory wound. Like the invisible war, this, in itself, does not hurt. Unlike the war, it is decidedly visible and absolutely disgusting. As its name suggests, it is a large suppurating wound which moves about, apparently of its own volition, from place to place and person to person. No one ever knows where it will appear next. Sometimes it appears on a newsboy's forehead or a senator's hand or (and this is embarrassing) on a dowager's thigh during a dinner party. It may also appear on things: on monuments, for example, or much frequented public buildings. Or it may simply station itself in a hitherto tranquil portion of the sky. It does not hurt anyone on whom it appears. Its coming is painless, as is its departure. If it has any conscious intent at all, it must surely intend to be, not a thing felt, but a thing seen. For, believe me, it is repellant to behold, and some sensitive people who have gazed upon it are now incurably insane.

The White Chapter

In this part of the story you wake up and find that everything is white. Morning and evening alike, the sky will be washed by searchlights. Stout women in aprons will glide past both sides of your bed carrying plates of dumplings. The knives will be sheathed in wool, the icepick embedded in cotton. When you cry, your tears will spread like cream around oatmeal. Nothing will be stained, nothing spotted. With your toes in plaster, like capped teeth, you will cross streets of crude rubber. So you do not skid into unmarked pits, the miners will scatter salt in your path. Nothing you meet with will be harsh. Strangers will hand their words to you wrapped in flour, and you will sift them grain by grain until the vowels lose their accents. You will discover the secret of stones, that stones are really made of hair coiled tightly upon itself. And you will learn how to unfasten the hair of stones until a stone flows soft as linen. From then on, nothing will pass away. You will stare at your pale, swollen belly as though it were the moon. The suicides leaping from the windows of office buildings will hang in the air like suspended loaves of bread. The farmboy brought before the firing squad will have the white handkerchief painted indelibly upon his eyes.

Staring

The way she kept staring.

The way her hands had nothing else in the world to do.

If you explained all the possible reasons why.

If she understood all the possible reasons why.

The way the daylight had been murdered.

That it was here and not some other place.

That it was this other place.

That it was not you and that you therefore could sympathize.

Did you remember her name?

The way she kept staring.

Coming there with one of her left fingernails broken.

Her collar standing up ungracefully, her coat thrown on in haste.

Because they thought she was trying to set her mind back.

When in truth her heels had already erased where her toes had been.

The turnings that turn directly into the wind.

Those the wind could take to meet you head on.

Suppose a man vacations in Hawaii and the day after he mails his Christmas cards he dies of a stroke on the beach, and the day after he is buried you receive a Christmas card signed by his own hand.

Suppose a charwoman in a high government office overhears conspiring generals plot to seize power with the aid of a hideous weapon.

Suppose you had decided not to drive down to the drug store or had come back into the room just one moment after the telephone had stopped ringing.

How it weighs on you.

Trying to rearrange, trying to foretell.

If that face, with its expression, were turned into a root,
   cooked, and served on a platter, and you were forced to
   taste, would its taste be tart or pulpy?
And did anyone figure out why she never bothered to but-
   ton her coat with its big yellow buttons even though
The way she kept staring The way her hands had nothing
   else
The way her hands had nothing else to do If you explained
If you explained the reasons for it The way the
The way the daylight was murdered That it was here not
That it was here not some other place The way she kept
The way she kept staring That you would eventually
That you would eventually be involved

Assembling the Evidence

The man who threads solitude into his clothes
left, or so he told us, for the East.
One thing is sure: we saw him take off,
under mild sedation, yet looking happy
and reasonably clear-headed. We watched him
sitting in the windowseat of the plane
a crepe paper hat on his head (a gift from the stewardess),
rise above roof gardens frequented
by sadistic Prussian weight lifters,
into the euphoria of thinning oxygen.
Another thing is sure: a telegram
has confirmed that last Friday at 12:15
he checked out of a hotel in Osaka, again
apparently of sound mind and body.
He has not been heard of since, although
the Japanese are investigating the case
with their usual tact and efficiency.

We admit it not impossible
that he could have moved to the house of friends.
Often we had heard him speak
of friends who owned some celebrated cherry trees,
although now that we might need them
we cannot remember their names.
As yet, there are no grounds for believing anything.

Searching his apartment, which none of us
had visited before, we were struck
by its strange absence of furniture.
Whether he had the furniture recently removed
(as an old stain on the wall like a chair back
suggests but does not prove) or whether it was always thus,
we do not know. We found a yellowed photograph

of a dead niece feeding vine leaves to a deer,
a shelf of maimed alarm clocks,
a half-empty glass of iced tea (the ice melted)
set upon some old jokes looking damp and wan,
and a delicate bowl of pink crystal
containing a small assortment of button-hooks.

Against the kitchen wall at eye-level was a black box
resembling a fuse box, its door held by a padlock.
On the box the following instructions were pasted:
"Lock key inside the box when you are done. The box
is opened by the key inside the box which must be locked
at all times. For safety, keep
a sand bucket handy beside the box."
Except for the last, which was carefully observed,
these instructions were impossible to follow.

Believing the box might contain some evidence,
we forced it open, some of us with crowbars,
others with hairpins or axes, and others
with a blowtorch. When the hinges dropped
from the metal door (there were so many,
so uncommonly many hinges falling)
we found inside nothing but a pocket mirror
our labors had accidentally broken.
We stared for hours until an inspector
interrupted and asked us for a personal description
of the man (any moles, scars, identifying marks,
that sort of thing). We found we could not agree
on a single detail. We argued, shouted
—and fell silent. Far off, we heard
the sound the tides make, changing.

A Dream of Metals

It was then I dreamed
of small metal objects
tacks to secure
casters to run on

I sorted locks, hooks
bolts and brads
staples loaded in a staple gun

I fill a bureau drawer
with clamps, valves
little wheels, springs
of no known source
or use
which nag to be used

on which I cut myself
and my blood tastes
of copper, silver, and tin

It was then I dreamed
of small metal objects

hinges like cocoons
on the sides of doors
screws thirsty for wood
the hibernation of spikes
on the roadbed

The small metals
trembling as though magnetized
rise one by one

out of the houses they hold together
out of the girders
out of the floorboards
out of the wings of tables

rise up in a cloud / merging
returned to their ore in mid-air
while the cities below them
fall like folded paper

clips, iron filings
the fillings of teeth
sawteeth, tenpenny nails
nuts, pins, and cogs
the strips around the lids of coffee cans

ascending transfigured
like small angels toward the sun

The sky looks half-erased,
washed out.

On a park bench in the shadow
a woman sits
plucking the hair from her head.
Then she unrolls her face
the way she might unroll a stocking.
Only the head itself is left—
white
blank
an egg.
She leans back,
breaks the egg against the bench.

Now darkness can begin,
and soot, and plunder.

Night, Window, Wind

All night long the window
kept blowing open
bringing the last of the rain
to my pillow

letting the light deepen
along the ceiling
and the curtains run loose in
mild disorder

each time it blew open
I would awaken
to fasten the window but
it would not stay

again it would open
before I could sleep
until the morning grew wide
with thoughts of sleep

but the light seemed lighter
then than anywhere
and oh how the air was sweet
after the rain

Blackhawk

Passing the skyway just before dusk
under the clouds chewing themselves up
I was on a great boulevard cementing the suburbs with
with a shabby strip of brown grass between lanes
I noticed sparrows wheel
and then the first headlights of cars
wheeled across my eyes like heavy wheels
like optical illusions / even with eyes closed
I watch them wheel attached
to sinister engines.
I am driving a cab and this stranger gets in
gradually disguising himself as the upholstery
until just his key-chain is left and I'm at the end of Cicero
down a blind street and a gang of thugs
pops out with machine guns
from what I thought were empty garages
or tool-and-dye works. I smell oil spots
and rags drenched with turpentine on the floor.
I think of racketeers herded at gunpoint into
a garage, this garage maybe
what must they think just before after the last insult snarls—

A girl with a hair ribbon
is playing "The Blackhawk Waltz"
on an upright piano, the bass notes
fall slightly muffled as though swathed
in cotton. Or she is playing them inside her own body
and the lake is swathed in cotton,
the lake opens its jaws
vagrant lights stumble in and drown,
cities flow southerly into the slag heaps. My ears are cold.
These brute girders obstruct our feelings,
our marketing research, our pits where the grain sifts.

Pages from an Imaginary Dream Book

1

As I walked
I scattered
the fallen leaves

I forget
what followed

2

We entered the harbor
to the sound
of cannon firing

3

She laughed
as she imposed
the impossible task

"Do it," she said
and the command was not
"bravely" or "nobly"

"Do it sweetly," she said

4

The cry of owls
made him flee
to the foxes

until the foxes
had usurped
the house

even bit
each other's ears
in the room

where he
had expected to see
his parents sleep

5

This is a place
upon the plains of Hungary

where they will know you
although you are a stranger

they will feed you here
and bathe you

and twenty girls with red ribbons
will dance around you in pointed boots

Scavengers

The garbage men of Omaha
wear shabby clothes and long black gloves
sticky with fishbones and the fur of dead rats.

The rag men of the prairie towns
stuff sunlight into burlap bags
and announce their coming with a smell of horse
and grandfather's threat
that they'll cart bad boys to the dump.

The garbage cans shake their bones
in the fog at the end of sleep
and the nerves shinny up a slivered tree
to hide in a nest of pillows.

The scavengers come collecting ruins,
the dome of white marble
which cracks in the skull,
the old fear crawling
damp on the lettuce leaf,
the bullet found
in a loaf of bread.

Three Little Stories

The Library

I have been given a library of children's books which once belonged to a famous film critic. She has bound each book in dark blue bindings. The bindings are faintly aromatic. Not of leather, not of ink, but of herbs, spices. For into each volume is bound one of Pavlova's tea leaves.

The Recital

I am in Chicago, walking down Michigan Ave. It is winter. There is snow on the ground. It is early evening, the time people start going to concerts. I pass Orchestra Hall. It is brightly lighted. There are many people lined up at the box office and standing in the foyer. In the crowd I see a man selling newspapers from another city. I try to go toward him and buy a copy, but in the crush I am knocked to the sidewalk. I get up again, annoyed; so annoyed, I cannot keep my balance and I fall down again, this time into a snowbank. I feel the wetness beneath my neck. As I fall I brush against a man holding some handbills. One of them floats down to me. It is an advertisement for a duo-piano recital to be given next week by me and a girl I once knew in high school. We are billed as "31-year-old prodigies." I have not seen this girl for many years. No one has told me about this concert before.

The Globe

I am in an artists' coffeehouse. They are playing a word game. Everyone, when his turn comes round, must leap to the center of the room and utter a single syllable. The syllables must never be allowed to form a word. The purpose of the game is to try to prolong the sequence indefinitely. The game is played very rapidly. Everyone is sweating. Down the narrow stairs into the dim room walks a man carrying a lighted globe. The oceans glisten. Antarctica is blinding white. Each continent, each country, even each province, glows in its color—pink, yellow, orange, green. The light from the globe shines on the man's long blond hair. It is a theatrical wig. The light shines on the blue cape across his shoulders. Although it is of heavy material it seems almost translucent. The cape is wide. It glows. It fills the entire stairway. Everyone in the room is silent.

Appearances

From the top landing
I peer into the stairwell
and see the back of a hand
go down the banister
to the ground floor.
Dare I assume
there is more than a hand
on the staircase?
Can I suppose as much as
an attached body?
That rhythmic sound
fading away
is not necessarily feet.
Might it not be my neighbor
pounding nails
while heavy draperies
are noiselessly lowered upon him?

I have seen that neighbor
from time to time
from the waist up
sitting in his window.
I wave to him
as I walk by.
He must know by this time
who I am,
yet he never waves back.
I am getting angry: why
is he so aloof? just who
does he think he is
not to wave back?
This morning I saw him

walking along the street
with a woman dressed like a nurse.
He had no arms.
But I cannot accept that
as a reason
for not waving back.
For inside the house
he might wear an artificial arm
or at least a hook.
Perhaps I should ask
that nurse about it,
but would she know for sure
(since when I saw her
she was carrying
a blind man's cane)?

In the desert
of my consternations
you and your smile
bring the comfort of a ripe orange.
I unpeel it
with my fingers,
raise it to my mouth
and suck the juice, wincing slightly.
Then I spit out the seeds
and let the peelings fall
into the gutter.
I am left with
sticky fingers
and what has become of you?
What has become of your smile?
I look for you. I strike a match

and it bursts into moonlight.
It is too dark out
to find anything except
where I am now,
and I keep losing myself.

I am lost in thought.
I am falling into the Hudson
with a cement block
tied to my left foot. It is impossible
to wave for help.
Didn't I tell you
I'm an amputee?
I near
the surface of the Hudson.
If it is not frozen over
I shall drop to the bottom.
It is frozen over.
I drop through a hole in the ice.
A hand crawls back up the banister
covered with blood.
Is it my hand
or someone else's?
If it is somebody else's
whose is it? If mine,
what is it doing on the stair?

The Face Asleep

The face asleep
in the bureau drawer
is my face on
another occasion
—not now.

Does the drawer have
knobs or a handle?
I don't know. I forget.

I forget, if I ever knew,
what color the face is,
although for a long time
I have known I await it.

Sometimes I think
the face is blue
as the night I dream of it
or blue as the morning
I will wear it
or blue as the paper
which lines the drawer.
Then I think it must be silver
as the mothballs in the drawer,
or brown as all four sides
of the drawer.
It may be black as an empty slate
or red, but not from rage.

It has never screamed,
it has never needed screaming.
It is the smooth face

before it finds its tears
or after the banishment
of cruelty.
It sleeps,
but does not fade away
as I do when I sleep.
It knows what it knows
without having to look.

Secure in its drawer (but which?),
with either pearl knobs
or an iron handle, it rests
serene as a color I cannot name.

Although I am not always sure
just where it is,
I know it will be there for me
when its time has come
—and its time will come.

The State

On the map of New York
I show you a place
called Stone Arabia.

"A curious image," you say.

I am gone. I wander
beneath marble palm trees
where petrified camels kneel.
They are the same camels that guard
a Shriners' Temple,
awkwardly rendered, with closed eyes,
of gray stone mottled
with mica flakes.

The snow is falling
upon Stone Arabia,
the elephants paling
as they pause before
a Dutch Reformed Church
which may not be there
either.

You say, "When I was little
White Plains
was what fascinated me.

"I saw it
as a prairie of chalk
or whitewash
stretching for three states
in every direction

"and nothing upon it
—no tree, no footprint, no drop of water—
except
in the distance
a single telephone pole
with wires chittering faintly
like seven-year locusts."

I say, "I have been
to White Plains.
It is
as you say it is,
a sterile place, yet
also a refuge
almost untouched
by human concerns
where no one need feel
responsible for anything.
There is nothing to look at
but a man can at least
keep his eyes open
without shame or hurting."

And you say, "Take me
to the minarets
of Stone Arabia.
You see it
as statuary,
whereas for me it is
not a town but a canyon
where rocks have eroded
into a thousand shapes

including the shapes
I imagined there."

I interrupt, "That being so,
perhaps we are there now."
You say, "Yes,
we are there perhaps."
"Or," I say, "we may be
somewhere else."
"Yes, somewhere else," you say.
"Or," I begin, "each of us
may be
in a separate place."
And you conclude,
"Or in the same place
separately."

Some Things That He Does

He never gets enough sleep. In the morning his eyes are no different than the dirty dishes stacked in the sink. It pleases him to pretend that his buttocks are apples, that his knees are hardboiled eggs. But where is the water that could cleanse his eyes?

He has built for himself a tent of stinking fish scales. Even the cats stay away from that smell. But he pitches his tent and breathes it all in, as though preparing to hear a cry for help. Whose? he wonders. Maybe mine?

The cockroaches are clever. When someone turns on the light, they hide along the edges of things and pretend to be woodwork. But he has painted all the walls pure white and they can be instantly detected. As they crawl they leave behind a trail of filth which glows in the dark like the lights of the cables of a distant bridge. That starts him worrying. What if tomorrow, he thinks, all the roaches turned albino? How could he catch them then?

4

He has bought a ticket for a play about the history of the Chippewa Indians. He has never seen a play on that subject before. He does not know what to expect. With Ibsen, for example, he always knows what to expect. Even if all the characters in Ibsen should come out wearing feathers in their hair and loincloths he would know what to expect. If William Archer had translated this he would have said, not "Indians," but "Red Indians," that being the British term to distinguish these Indians from that other kind in India. In America when we say "Indians," we always know what we mean. Or do we?

5

On his way to work he steals crumbs of dry bread from the birds' feeding station. He doesn't like the taste much. It's like croutons in onion soup without the onion soup. But it opens his eyes to what animals eat. A whole new world to eat starts cooking in his head. He dreams of catfood, of dog biscuits, of birdseed. Is it possible, he wonders, that birdseed has the same effect upon the brain as morning glory seeds? His head reels. Really?

6

His head reels. He cuts a door inside it and lets out a troupe of Scottish dancers. He blushes from head to toe, having been brought up to believe that the pun is the lowest form of humor. But now he thinks it may be mightier than the sword. He feels his toes starting to chuckle. What the hell! Why not? He chuckles all over.

Health Poem

I do not think I have good health.
I have interrupted sleep.
I spit consciousness.

Sunshine may promote bladders,
reduce buzzing in the ears, tune them,
but my leg has gone numb
while I try to remember where I put my
steady breathing.
I'm on the lookout for ruptures.

I am ill in a strange land
with a large strange language stuck in my throat.
I am stricken with verbs of suspicion.
Human relationships ravage me
like an epidemic of glottal stops.

"Do you have hives? Shingles?" "A limp wrist?"
"A stiff upper lip?"
Sometimes I think I've had the hiccups
for forty days and forty nights.

In a severe state of shock
even when I'm dancing
I live with conjectures pumped into my veins,
I'm bothered by dizzy spells and bed sores.

An unidentifiable allergy
is prowling and scratching inside my skin.
Day by day my ailments
are gradually made known to me
like a stage set upon which
a curtain rises.

A Convalescence

A terror of nightingales stuck in my throat.
Miles away my hands hung limp
On hooks in a meat market freezer.
My eyes were marbles rolling in the circle
Of the night-light.
                    All night long the night bird sang
Lonely in the ranges of my skeleton
And from the measures of its music
Stray words brushed my forehead with hot wings:
Gorgonzola, noseflute, bastinado, turpentine,
And a list of crimes I could not quite make out.
My mouth bobbed open in attempted speech, but the fierce
Thoughts foundered in a rage of parenthesis.

2

At last I grew content with myself,
Pleased to hear the currents of my blood:
A waterfall in the distance, or
An underground river heard dimly beneath the lawn.
The window opened, the world
Trickled in around the medicines.
The befuddled wasp trapped in the ward
Flew out between the curtains.

3

With the lessening of pain
The bandages fell like rain water.
The nurse brought long-stemmed roses to my bedside.
"I was wrapped in the moon," I said, "in the winter moon."
My hand moved across the sheets
Like a thawing brook.

The Casualties

The voice on the radio
Is naming the casualties.
Their name is "The Casualties."

Commas invade the tabletop.
The doorknob is a human fist.
Corners of rooms
Fold me in like envelopes.
I vanish inside my mouth.

We have buried a music stand
Instead of a tyrant.
The nightfall squats on the roof like lard.

Daily Luncheon Intention

"A bowl of chocolate experience," I say
and as the counterman fills my order
I busy myself with instances:
no, not "The Hearth Shop"
or the safari through a broom;
not even the sanctuary
for the whooping crane
where the thunder of breadcrumbs
is the only diversion.

No, if I must be a beast
let me be dingy and tumescent
like a bison or a solecism.
Sometimes I may open
a disgusting yellow eye
to shout, "Adventure! Adventure!
Soda water!"
and chase the fire trucks
or dig for fleas.

Smirks creep from mouths
on six clammy legs
for Horror is a pale man with glasses
loitering by the pinball machine.
I, too, am a pale man with glasses
loitering by a pinball machine
and so, I begin to think, are you.
Even though each of us has his own pinballs
relations are strained.

Every time the refrigerator opens
a pregnant woman falls out
and it is less discussed than the prizefights.
Worse:
whenever these customers bite their hamburgers
at that precise instant a baby screams.
I know there may be explanations for this,
it makes me nervous nevertheless.

The Man at the Campground

When I was about your age, he said,
I was working up at Sequoia
and when I had a vacation coming
I shaved myself and collected my pay
and jumped on the little motor scooter I had then

I wore just an old shirt
boots and levis
all I packed
was a toothbrush and an extra pair of shorts

I didn't know where I was going
I just took off

I wound up at the Grand Canyon

The first time I saw it
it was so big
I had to step back
before I could look at it again

I had me one hell of a good time
it only cost four dollars for gas
—except in Barstow it was so dry
they charged me a dime for a glass of water

Hurricane

At Gold Beach, Oregon,
light and power were gone.
I had to have gas
piped to my car
from the Shell storage tank.
I slept the night
in Eureka, dreamless.
The morning brought me
back to rain.

When I reached the turnoff
for the redwood groves
I chose to risk
roads cobbled with leaves
and fallen branches
until there was no more road,
just a space between trees.
A car pulled beside me.
"Turn around," the man shouted,
"there's a big one down ahead."

At Petaluma I stopped
for coffee and rolls
in a little bakery.
All words spoken
said storm.

It was only when I came
to the freeway near home
where the road seemed to balance
on the back of the wind
and the pavement lurched

in spasms of rain
and Mount Tamalpais reared up
like a month of thunder
over pale walls of suburbs
crouched in a ring,
only then did I remember
to be afraid.

You said, "Let's stop somewhere for a snack."
So we met for lunch at the La Brea Tarpits.

But the coffee was so strong
It caught in our hair
And the licorice held on to our hands
With its teeth
And hung itself on our bodies
Like a rented tuxedo.

We kept digging up the bones
Of dead trucks and ex-Follies girls.

So at evening
When the searchlights turned on their bugs,
We hailed a passing saber-toothed tiger,
Held hands, took a deep breath,
And plunged into the freeway.

When our bodies were found
We were five days off Anaheim
And the end was not yet in sight.

The Streetcars

A little night music
    late radio among the trees / the trees
have blossomed since yesterday
    and shine like the hammered work
       of silversmiths
as the last streetcars weave between them
    lighting them
the way a mind drunk on wine
                 waltzes
    from fact to fact
          fitfully
endowing the world
    in bits and pieces
      with a dizzy glow
which will not come this way again tonight

On the Road to the Eye Hospital

When we get to the eye hospital
you will say,
"Now there's a sight for sore eyes."
Then it will be Skipper's turn
to say a four-letter word
such as "Fibber McGee"
and Miss Butterworth will serenade us
with "The Sweetheart of Sigma Chi."

On the road to the eye hospital
we shall wave to the walrus
and wrap sheets around moppets
who wet the bed.
We shall pretend not to notice
that Butch keeps staring
at ladies' undies.
You will lecture to us
on how to steal hubcaps.

When we get to the eye hospital
Sis will feed Skipper to the snapping **turtles.**
So we'll have room in the car
to drive you back home.
Miss Butterworth will be drunk
on root beer and oatmeal
but no matter what she sings
she always remembers
to replace the naughty words with blanks
as in the song "My sister has a white **horse,**
My —— —— has an ——."

Place a custard stand in a garden
or in place of a custard stand
   place a tumbled-down custard stand
in place of a tumbled-down custard stand
   place miniature golf in a garden
   and an advertisement for miniature golf
     shaped for no apparent reason
     like an old Dutch windmill
in place of a swamp
   place a swamp

       or a pizzeria called the Tower of Pizza
        sporting a scale model
         of the Tower of Pisa
       or a water tower resembling
        a roll-on deodorant
       or a Dixie Cup factory
        with a giant metal Dixie Cup on the roof

In place of wolverines, rabbits, or melons
   place a vulcanizing plant
in place of a deer
   place an iron deer
   at a lawn furniture store
   selling iron deer
     Negro jockeys
     Bavarian gnomes
     and imitation grottoes
     with electric Infants of Prague
in place of phosphorescence
   of marshy ground at night
     place smears of rubbish fires
in place of brown water with minnows
   place brown water

gigantic landlords
in the doorways of apartment houses
which look like auto showrooms
auto showrooms which look like diners
diners which look like motels
motels which look like plastic chair covers
plastic chair covers which look like
plastic table covers which look like plastic bags

the mad scientist of Secaucus
invents a plastic cover
to cover the lawn
with millions of perforations
for the grass to poke through

In place of the straight lines of grasses
    place the straight lines of gantries
in place of lights in the window
    place lighted refineries
in place of a river
    place the road like a slim pair of pants
        set to dry beside a neon frankfurter
in place of New Jersey
    place a plastic New Jersey

on weekends a guy has nothing to do
except drive around in a convertible
counting the shoe stores
and thinking of screwing
    his date beside him
    a faintly bilious look
    perpetually on her face

Paper Clip

Liquor finish
(Liquid finish)
Steel wire   diameter

Tiger brand
"Millions daily"
Curve and repeat   and

Liquid steel
Tiger wire
.036″ daily

A Dance of Definitions Around Their Words

in opposition to
in reverse
in the wrong direction

a return
a parry
a boxer's parry

a person who enumerates
a token
a shelf where goods are placed for inspection

an imitation coin
a piece of ivory, metal, wood
a parry in a circular direction

a friend's name
Scotch knowledge

the range of vision

nickname
or dialect

to recognize an heir

an extremity
an old-timer
an adept

the foot of a hawk
the pointer on a clock
a bundle of tobacco leaves

a worker
a cowboy
applause

all company assembled
to pass along
to furl a sail

power
custody
help

a pledge of marriage
a game of cards
the measure of the height of horses

Weather Report

The parking meters stand in line
waiting to have their pictures taken

The river at the end of every street
has been made invisible
except when the smell rises
(which is not pleasant)
it is not pleasant
the stink of the dead rat
on the rampage inside the wall
it is retribution
for having dressed the cat
in drag as a dog

Oh pretty pretty says the apple in one lunch bag
to the *My orchard is short of*
a peach like you in the other

I think of you as a tangerine
I think of Sol Hurok
sending caviar to the music critics
a pomegranate takes my breath away
to see so sexual a foodstuff
can it be pleasant?

The barges keep floating by
as regular as Christmas

Meanwhile the temperature in Miami Beach
rises like a broker gaining weight
mildew is apparent in Amarillo
(it is not pleasant)

Tom Thumb's wedding party
and the patent medicine man selling snakeroot
float down the Mississippi
in a burlesque comedian's gunboat shoes
candy butchers what of the night?
Persephone falls like a house afire
into French Lick, Indiana

Precipitation Monday

It's past player piano time and I'm
still eating the left wings
jammed into the steerage.
The brand label is "incest"
once upon a time known as hex.

At six o'clock a maiden will glide
into a pavilion of peppermint leaves.
I will watch her while our neighbor's rowboat
goes mad with the piano in the steerage
and blares like a goat.

What better friend than a pianola?
I know one. It's steeplechase,
the beautiful, lonely, wingèd time
we labeled incest on a rainy Monday
blue as the hour of player pianos.

The world's a spare room
I once thought was a bathing suit
as it once was a rowboat.
Always the pavilion
shelters the Old Dutch Cleanser girl.

A knife parting raisins.
They flicker into Christian Science
or smile resigned in their net
when the catalogue lisps the piano rolls
from the time of trench warfare.

Knowing too little about labels
and thinking too much about whiskers
with castanets attached, I sneak
through the spare room to throttle the totem
and praise the morning of raisins.

Look, I open my flashlight.

For Sure

Your coziness has spilled through my fingers,
feathers flying.
We had wanted to get cozy.

The feathers first
piled up in the corners
of the Medical College
we tried to fight our way out of.
Through keyholes we spied the feet of cadavers
stretched on a formica table
or a steel fact.

The fact is, we think that beyond those feet was
nothing,
that the rest of the bodies had already fallen
into the Vanishing Machine.
Feathers were starting to float by:
loose feathers,
bees,
blizzards.

Downtown, four overturned autos
sprawled helpless as turtles.
The pillars of the savings bank
writhed like jellyfish, purple and translucent.
A bus stuck its rump
toward the air. I longed to replace it
with twelve bellboys in fancy blue
trotting down the street in unison,
a furnished villa on their backs.

"Is this only a figment?" you cried. "Or flagellation?"
Then we turned the corner into homecoming.
It wore the face of a boiled potato.
Famine's full wingspan was nailed to the wall.
The frying pan's look was one great gape.

"Just five years . . . fortune," I panted. You repeated
what you had said. Or had seen:

The feeble parrot stumbles, falls,
fidgets helpless now
beneath the weight of its own green egg.
It's a bomb,
for sure.

Quotient

The increased quotient of pain
as computed in hot curled wires
shines at night above the entrance ramp

a handshake with a certain pressure
was the agreed-upon signal
fingers weighted by rings
begin to press multi-colored buttons
arranged in a scale of ascending severity
reminiscent of the hand
holding the sponge soaked in chloroform
or the pellets they swear are only mothballs

at night the soldiers imagine ways to get even
back home
women on the rope bridge
line up, submissive to the avalanche
each time it happens our disquiet grows
bees die poisoned in their hives
we suspect things but hesitate
to write them down / for fear of punishment
or do even we find it hard to believe
such charges could be true?

never doubting the announced goals
the nurse steadies the patient's arm
the secretary's left heel disappears
into the private office
the rest of her body cannot yet be seen
through the glass door
she brings the latest calculations

looking through half of his bifocals
he seemed almost relieved that it had been done
now we await more tangible results

Toward an Inventory of the American Image

A barber pole painted to resemble
a draped American flag
a pasture gate painted to resemble
an American flag unfurled

An American flag rising
over a sun rising
over a river in New Hampshire
to illustrate the words
"By the dawn's early light"

An American eagle and shield rising
over a view of the Mohawk River
and a farmer in a field
and a ship upon the waters
and a train along the ridges
to illustrate the words
"American Commerce and Industry"

A wooden statue of George Washington
said to have adorned the Bowling Green
later pulled down / later set up
to adorn the first Washington Arch
later pulled down
found again adorning a tobacco shop in Harlem
later pulled down
later sold at auction
not seen again for seventy years

A wooden statue of Abraham Lincoln
with real buttons and leather boot straps
and coattails of painted cardboard
a wooden statue of Abraham Lincoln
said to have been carved by a Negro slave

A weathervane in the shape of Uncle Sam
a weathervane in the shape of the Angel Gabriel

A weathervane in the shape of Chief Tammany of the
    Indians
who made the treaty with William Penn
a treaty never signed and never broken
Chief Tammany of the Indians
who kept the peace
who gave his name to the American rebels
who because the redcoats called themselves
Sons of St. Andrew / Sons of St. George
called themselves the Sons of St. Tammany
because they were free
and honorable men

Tangerines
Against a white glaze
Shining
Beside the milk pitcher

Tangerines
Which seemed to call
Against a white glaze
A frank proposition

The voice
Along the subway tracks
Which seemed to call:
Nothing stays

The voice
Along the subway tracks
Which seemed to call:
Nothing stays

Festivals
We barely remember
Have we kept
The faith

Shining
Beside the milk pitcher
The gift of apples
Against a white glaze

The voice
Is in truth a fire
Along the subway tracks
Or kindness

Tangerines
Against a white glaze
Shining
Beside the milk pitcher

The voice
Along the subway tracks
Which seemed to call:
Nothing stays

Which seemed to call
Festivals
We barely remember
Have we kept

The gift of apples
Nothing stays
Festivals
Along the subway tracks

The gift of apples
Or kindness
Is in truth a fire
A frank proposition

Where You Are

This is where you are.
Please note.
You are reading a poem
Beginning, "This is where you are."
Now get up
And walk three times around the room,
Then drink from a faucet
(If you can find a faucet).
Do not use a glass.
Stick your mouth directly
Into the stream of water.
Feel the water,
Its coldness, its wetness.
If there is no faucet near you
Or if the water is not potable,
Observe sky
And whatever may fill it
(In the margin you may write
The names of three things
You see in the sky)
And try to decide
Whether our present condition
Is best described
As peace or war.
What is the difference
Between this and "this"?
Please take note
Of where you are.
Did you really walk around the room
As requested?
Have you written anything in the margin?
Are you sitting, standing,

Or reclining?
You are reading a poem
Which will end,
"Of all this is."
But you are not there yet.
You are here.
You are getting there.
Now explain precisely
What the point
Of all this is.

COLOPHON: The poems in this book are set in Linotype Baskerville, a typeface dating from the eighteenth century. The cutting used here was produced from a complete font cast from the original matrices found at Paris in 1929. The printing is by Heritage Printers, Inc., on Warren's Olde Style antique wove paper, and the binding cloth is a product of Columbia Mills. The design is by Gary Gore.

Pitt Poetry Series

The Invention of New Jersey
by Jack Anderson

As a poet Jack Anderson is more interested in diversity than in artificially maintaining a single style. He regards the poet as a sort of chameleon adapting himself to the demands of each new set of poetic materials. He is very much affected by the place in which he happens to be, by its appearance, its tone, its pace, and its climate (both physical and emotional).

DIANE WAKOSKI: "I like his poetry because it takes me into another world, one where wit conquers the pain of inadequacy and the sur-beautiful covers up the dingy hopelessness of reality. The test of a poet, for me, is whether or not he can take you into his own world, his own creation, and fascinate you enough to stay there a while and savor the poems. I think Jack Anderson's poetry is a true record of an imagination."

JOHN PERREAULT: "Jack Anderson is one of the most talented poets I know. I have followed his work for some time now with great delight and with great admiration for his wit and his seriousness. . . . The poems in *The Invention of New Jersey* are funny, beautiful, intelligent (a rarity!) and terribly moving."

Jack Anderson, a graduate of Northwestern University, received his Master's degree from Indiana University. He acted with the San Francisco Arena Theater and the San Francisco Shakespeare Festival, 1963, has been a drama critic, and currently works for *Dance Magazine*.

University of Pittsburgh Press